HISTORY MAKERS

ANCIENT GREEKS

CLARE CHANDLER

ILLUSTRATED BY JESSICA CURTIS

Wayland

HISTORY MAKERS

Notes for teachers

History Makers uses a wide range of exciting contemporary sources — quotations, letters, paintings and artefacts — to build up detailed and informative portraits of people who made important contributions both to their own time and to the way we live now.

This book:

- features important figures from all areas of life in ancient Greece — science and technology, the arts, architecture, sport, warfare, education and health;

- presents contemporary reactions to changes and innovations;

- focuses on the make-up of ancient Greek society and the changes and developments that occurred within it;

- emphasizes the importance of ancient Greek achievements for modern life.

First published in 1994 by
Wayland (Publishers) Ltd
61 Western Road, Hove,
East Sussex BN3 1JD,
England

Copyright 1994 Wayland (Publishers) Ltd

Series editor: Katie Roden
Series designer: Tracy Gross
Book designer: Marilyn Clay

**British Library Cataloguing
in Publication Data**

Chandler, Clare
Ancient Greeks. – (History Makers Series)
I. Title II. Curtis, Jessica III. Series
938

ISBN 0 7502 1503 8

Typeset by Dorchester Typesetting Group Ltd,
England
Printed and bound in Italy by Lego

Picture acknowledgements:
Ancient Art & Architecture Collection (Ronald Sheridan) 6, 7, 9, 10, 11, 14, 15, 17, 22, 23, 26, 29, 30, 31, 33, 34, 35, 36, 39, 41, 42; British Museum 18, 38; Michael Holford Photographic 13, 21, 24 (British Museum), 25, 27, 37; Wayland Picture Library 19 (both).

Contents

Words in **bold** in the text can be found in the Glossary on page 44.

H o m e r

c. 8 5 0 - 7 5 0 B C

'The wisest of all the Greeks.'

The **philosopher** Heraclitus said this about Homer, even though very little was known about the man. All we know about him was that he was a wandering poet and that he was probably blind. However, his two great poems, the *Iliad* and the *Odyssey*, are the proof of his brilliance.

The *Iliad* tells the story of the war between the Greeks and the people of Troy. This war began when a woman called Helen fell in love with the Trojan prince, Paris, and went to live with him in Troy.

This is a picture on a vase of Menelaus recapturing his wife, Helen, after the end of the Trojan War. Helen was famous for her beauty, and it was said that her face 'launched a thousand ships'. What do you think that means?

6

However, Helen was already married to Menelaus, the brother of the Greek king. The Greeks, determined to get Helen back, **besieged** Troy for ten years. Finally, they tricked the Trojans, destroyed the city, and captured Helen.

This vase shows Circe offering her drugged wine to Odysseus. But he has been given a magic herb by the god Hermes to protect him.

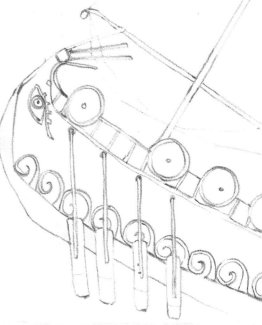

One of the Greek leaders was called Odysseus. It took him ten years to get home after the sacking of Troy. The *Odyssey* tells the story of his adventures on the way to Troy and on his return. Odysseus was famous for his cunning mind and there are stories of how he outwitted several monsters, including the one-eyed giant, Cyclops. Once, when Odysseus' men were walking through the woods, they came across the house of the goddess Circe (pronounced Sur'-see). She welcomed them in, but put a drug in their wine. Then:

'She struck them with her wand and drove them into her pig pens, and they took on the look of pigs, with the heads and voices and bristles of pigs, but the minds within them stayed as they had been before.'

However, Odysseus won Circe over and she finally freed his men. As well as being wonderful stories, the *Iliad* and the *Odyssey* tell us a great deal about the lives and beliefs of the early Greeks.

7

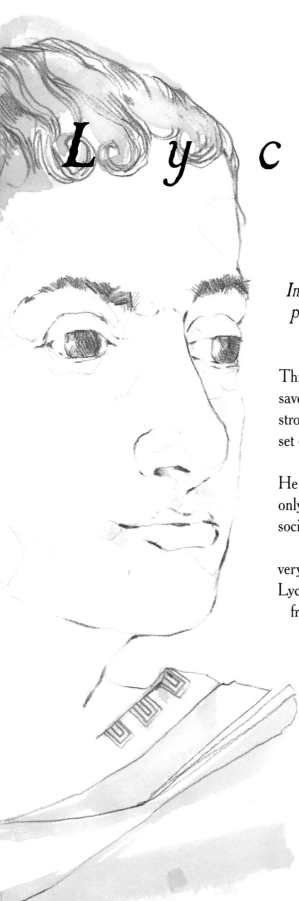

Lycurgus

c. ninth century BC

In order to expel arrogance, envy, crime, luxury ... wealth and poverty, Lycurgus persuaded the citizens to pool all the land and redistribute it afresh.

Through changes such as this, the writer Plutarch says that Lycurgus saved the southern Greek state of Sparta from collapse and made it very strong. Lycurgus is believed to have set up a whole new government and set of laws.

Before he came to power, Lycurgus had travelled widely in Greece. He had seen other states become weak because the people in power were only interested in wealth and luxurious living. Lycurgus felt that a fairer society where all the people were happy would make a stronger state.

In Sparta there were some very rich people, but most people were very poor. The cities were full of homeless people begging in the streets. Lycurgus therefore made sure that everyone had an equal plot of land, from which they were expected to grow a certain amount of food and give it to the state. Then he insisted that all the men eat their meals together in a hall so that they would not waste their time:

'... lying at table on expensive couches ... fattened up in the dark like gluttonous animals ... giving free rein to every craving and excess which demanded lengthy slumbers, warm baths, plenty of rest, and, in a sense, daily nursing.'

The only money Lycurgus allowed the people to use was iron bars. In this way gold and silver became worthless, poverty was reduced and there was very little crime.

8

A statue of Lycurgus at Sparta, holding his decrees.

Children were considered to be the property of the whole state, not just of their parents. Sadly for the parents, if a baby was born weak it was left to die on the mountainside. Children were trained not to be fussy eaters, not to be afraid of the dark, and not to have temper tantrums.

In the eighth century BC, Sparta had conquered its neighbouring state of Messenia. The Messenians were never very happy under Spartan rule and rebelled against it. It was important, therefore, for Sparta to have a strong army. For this reason, all boys were trained to become soldiers. From the age of seven, boys joined a troop of soldiers. They went barefoot and naked except for a single cloak and they were only allowed to have about two baths a year. They slept on beds made from reeds, although in winter they could add some thistledown to their beds to make them warmer. They were given very little to eat and were encouraged to steal food. But if one of them was caught stealing he was whipped soundly – for being an unskilled thief!

We can tell that this figure of a woman running is an athlete from Sparta because of her short tunic.

Women were trained to be fit as well, and competed in games. Unlike women in other parts of Greece who wore flowing robes, they wore short tunics. They were not allowed to wear make-up or jewellery.

When the Greeks founded Sparta in the ninth century BC, they treated the people who were already living there like slaves. They called these people *helots* and made them farm the land, so that the Spartans could spend their time training to be soldiers. According to the philosopher Plato, there was a tradition called the *krypteia*, in which young Spartan men were sent out into the countryside at night with a dagger to kill as many *helots* as they could. But Plutarch believed that this must have been popular after Lycurgus left Sparta because, he says:

'I would not attribute such a foul exercise as the krypteia to Lycurgus.'

Lycurgus, pleased with his city, said that he was going to **Delphi** to consult the **oracle**, and made the city leaders promise that none of the laws would be changed until he returned. At Delphi he starved himself to death to make sure that the laws were never changed.

Sparta remained strong and well ordered for 500 years. However, this had only been made possible by harsh measures – slavery, killing of the weak and a concentration on warfare, which left no time for more gentle occupations like art and literature.

The Spartans were famous for their toughness, strength and military skill, and the expression 'Spartan' still has the meaning 'simple' or 'basic'.

A statue of a Spartan warrior from the sixth century BC.

11

S a p p h o

c. 612 – 580 BC

'*Sappho, who was something wonderful; at no period within memory has any woman been known who in any, even the least, degree could be compared to her for poetry.*'

This was the opinion of Strabo, a historian and geographer who lived six hundred years after Sappho. Her poetry has continued to inspire people and influence other poets for almost 3,000 years.

This woman is playing a kithara, an instrument similar to a lyre. Women would often play the kithara, lyre or harp while they sang or chanted poetry.

OTHER POETS

Homer
– see pages 6–7.

Hesiod (eighth century BC) – an early Greek poet. He wrote about his life as a peasant farmer in *Works and Days.*

Anacreon (c.570–490 BC) – a poet who wrote about love, wine and the pleasures of life.

Apollonius Rhodius (born c.300 BC) – a poet from Alexandria who wrote a four-book poem called the *Argonautica.*

Sappho lived on the island of Lesbos. It was an unusual place because the women who lived there had much more freedom than in other parts of Greece. In general, Greek women had no say in politics. They were in the power of their husbands if they were married. If they were unmarried they had to have a male guardian. The husband or guardian controlled their lives and their property. Girls did not go to school, but were taught how to be wives and mothers at home. However, on Lesbos women were more independent and better educated and, as a result, Sappho was able to make the most of her talent.

This town on the island of Lesbos has clearly grown up around its ancient buildings.

Lesbos was a beautiful island, peaceful and **fertile**, and famous for its oil and wine. Sappho was the leader of a group of women who would spend their time sitting in the shade of the olive groves or wandering in the hills amongst the fragrant wild herbs, composing poetry or singing it to the accompaniment of the **lyre** or harp.

Sappho wrote her poems on papyrus books. These were long scrolls of paper made from the stalks of papyrus, a water plant. Many of her poems have survived only in parts, because the papyrus was later used for other things. Bits of her poems have been found torn up and stuffed into the mouths of **mummified** crocodiles, though it is not clear why! However, professional singers would copy the songs and poems and sing them wherever Greek was spoken, so Sappho's fame spread and her poems were handed down from one generation to the next.

The rest of Sappho's life is a bit of a mystery. We know from her poems that she was married and had a daughter called Cleis. It also seems that another famous poet, Alcaeus, was in love with her. He wrote:

'... violet-weaving, pure, soft-smiling Sappho, I want to say something but shame deters me.'

DATE CHART

c.612 BC
Sappho is born.

594 BC
Solon is appointed archon at Athens.

580 BC
Sappho dies.

14

But Sappho is said to have been in love with a handsome boatman called Phaon. The story is that he did not love her and, in despair, she killed herself. On the island of Levkás, part of the cliff is still known as 'Sappho's Leap'. This is the spot where Sappho is believed to have thrown herself into the sea. In ancient Greece, criminals sentenced to death were thrown into the sea at this place. Birds were tied to their legs and arms and they were covered with feathers, to break the force of their fall. If they survived, they were pardoned.

An ancient coin from the island of Lesbos, showing the head of Sappho.

During her lifetime, Sappho was known throughout Greece as 'the Poetess' and her head was engraved on local coins, which was a very rare honour for a woman. Her influence has been great throughout the ages and the style and rhythms of her poems have been copied by many poets. Even in Victorian times, the poet Swinburne wrote of her:

'Sappho is simply nothing less – as she is certainly nothing more – than the greatest poet who ever was at all.'

15

S o l o n

c. 638 – 558 BC

'Often the wicked grow rich, while good
people starve;
Yet I would never exchange my state for
theirs,
My virtue for their gold.
For mine will stay,
While riches change their owner every day.'

This is a verse from one of Solon's poems. He was one of the famous **Seven Wise Men** and was chosen by the people of Athens to be **archon** at a very difficult time. A few men had control of all the wealth of the city, while most people were poor and heavily in debt. Many of them had had to promise that they would become the property of the person from whom they borrowed money; if they could not pay it back they became slaves or were sold to foreigners. Many parents were forced to sell their children or to go into **exile**.

16

When Solon took charge, he cancelled all debts and decreed that no one could be made a slave in payment of a debt. Then he changed the laws of the city. They had been drawn up by a **lawgiver** called Draco, and they were extremely harsh: someone could be condemned to death for stealing fruit and vegetables, or even for laziness! The laws were said to be written in blood instead of ink, and the expression 'Draconian' still describes laws that are very severe. Solon introduced much fairer laws, which were displayed on wooden blocks on the **Acropolis** for about a thousand years.

The Acropolis of Athens. Acropolis means 'high city' in Greek and it was a sacred part of the town, where temples were built. The temple in this photograph, the Parthenon, was built between 447–438 BC.

The land around Athens was very poor and could not produce enough food for all the people of the city. Solon encouraged people to make things to sell abroad in exchange for the food that they needed.

He also spurred his people on to war with the people of Megara. The Megarians had captured an island called Salamis that had once belonged to Athens, and Solon made a plan to recapture it. First a party of warriors sailed to a place near Salamis, where many Athenian women were having a festival in honour of a goddess. Then someone was sent to the island of Salamis pretending to be a **deserter** from the Athenian army. He told the Megarians that if they hurried they could catch the Athenian women at the festival and capture them. Meanwhile, the women had been replaced by Athenian soldiers disguised in women's robes, head-dresses and sandals. The soldiers danced on the beach like the women, their daggers hidden under their dresses. When the Megarians leapt out of their boats to capture the 'women', they were attacked by them and killed. The Athenians then sailed over to Salamis and recaptured the island.

Daggers, like the one carried by this warrior, were used by Solon's soldiers during the fight for Salamis.

DATE CHART

c.638 BC
Solon is born.

c.621 BC
Draco is appointed archon in Athens.

c.594 BC
Solon is appointed archon in Athens.

c.560 BC
Solon dies.

18

These coins from Athens show the goddess Athena (above) and her emblem, an owl (below). Solon greatly increased the wealth of the city.

Some of Solon's poems and sayings have survived, such as 'in great affairs you cannot please everyone'. But Solon is best known for having made Athens strong at a time of crisis and for bringing it closer to the **democracy** which has stood as a model for governments ever since.

OTHER STATESMEN

Lycurgus
– see pages 8–11.

Pericles (died 429 BC)
– a general and statesman who controlled Athens from about 460–429 BC. He was responsible for the temples on the Acropolis.

Themistocles
– see page 10.

Aeschylus

525 – 456 BC

'I brought my songs for a noble purpose from a noble source.'

Aeschylus wrote plays nearly two and a half thousand years ago, yet they are so interesting and powerful that they are still performed today. They were some of the first plays ever written. Theatre began as part of a Greek festival in honour of the god Dionysus. The festival was called the *Dionysia* and was held every year. It lasted for five days and it included sacrifices and processions as well as a drama competition.

This vase painting shows Dionysus, the god of wine, holding a grape vine. In Athens, drama competitions were held during the great spring festival to honour him.

The plays took place in an outdoor theatre. There were never more than three main actors in a play and they were all men, even playing the women's parts. They wore masks, which they changed to become other characters. The masks were made from stiffened paper or cork and had exaggerated expressions to suit the characters. Some of the theatres were huge, holding thousands of people, so everything had to be larger than life in order to be seen from the back seats. The main actors played on a raised stage and in front of them, on the ground, another group of actors, called the chorus, danced and sang and made comments on the story of the play.

There were two types of plays – tragedies and comedies. The tragedies were always about heroic figures and dealt with serious subjects such as war. The comedies were either about ordinary people or made fun of politicians and other famous people of the time. Sometimes the comedies made fun of the writers of the tragedies. In *The Frogs*, a comedy by Aristophanes, Aeschylus and another tragedian, Euripides, have a contest to decide who is the better playwright. Euripides accuses Aeschylus of boastful language and of babbling about whatever comes into his head:

DATE CHART

534 BC
First drama is staged at Athens.

525 BC
Aeschylus is born.

513 BC
The Persians invade Europe.

508 BC
Cleisthenes seizes power in Athens.

500–499 BC
Greek colonies revolt against Persian rule.

494 BC
The Persians suppress an Ionian revolt.

21

'Euripides: But I know him; I've read him!
His style is awful – loose, sloppy,
Undisciplined, grandiose,
Gross, affected…
Aeschylus: I won't take that from you …'

Ancient Greek masks had large mouths so that the actors could be heard. Do you think this bronze figure is of an actor in a tragedy or a comedy?

490 BC
The Persians invade the Greek mainland, but are defeated at the Battle of Marathon.

480 BC
The Persians, a play by Aeschylus, is performed.

479 BC
The Persians are defeated at the Battle of Plataea and leave Greece.

478 BC
Athens and other Greek states form The Delian League against the Persians.

458 BC
The Oresteia, a trilogy of plays by Aeschylus, is performed at the festival of Dionysus, and wins first prize.

460–457 BC
The Long Walls are built around Athens. The Acropolis is rebuilt.

456 BC
Aeschylus dies.

We know from various accounts of his life that Aeschylus had to leave Athens, although there are several possible reasons for this. One reason may have been his most famous plays, a **trilogy** called the *Oresteia*, about a man called Orestes who kills his mother. In the final play, Orestes is tormented by demons called Furies, who represent his dead mother's angry spirit.

22

It is said that when the play was first performed in Athens, the Furies appeared one by one and the audience was so frightened that children fainted and pregnant women gave birth to their babies. This might have been why Aeschylus had to leave Athens. But in the *Suda*, an ancient encyclopedia of literature, it says that Aeschylus:

'... went into exile in Sicily because the stage fell down when he was putting on a performance.'

However, the people of Athens liked Aeschylus' plays so much that they voted after his death to award a golden crown to whoever would stage one of his dramas. Aeschylus' death, unfortunately, would have been a better subject for a comedy than a tragedy. He was killed when a flying eagle dropped a tortoise on his head. It is thought that the eagle was looking for a rock on which to break open the shell of the tortoise, and mistook Aeschylus' bald head for one.

Ancient Greek theatres, like this one at Ephesus, held thousands of people. The circle in the middle was called the orchestra and it was where the chorus sang and danced. Apart from giving a good view, the semi-circle shape of the theatre was excellent for carrying the sound from the stage to the audience in the back rows.

OTHER PLAYWRIGHTS

Sophocles (496–406 BC) – of his 123 tragedies, only seven survive. These include *King Oedipus*, *Electra* and *Antigone*.

Euripides (c.480–406 BC) – a writer of tragedies, including *The Bacchae*. He was sympathetic towards women and poor people. He believed in democracy and hated war.

Aristophanes (c.450–380 BC) – a writer of comedies. His plays make fun of famous politicians, poets and philosophers. His best-known plays are *The Birds*, *The Frogs* and *Lysistrata*.

23

Pheidippides

c.515 BC – ?

'Men of Sparta, the Athenians ask you to help them, and not to stand by while the most ancient city of Greece is crushed and enslaved by a foreign invader.'

This is the message that Pheidippides ran 250 km to deliver. The Persians, people from the country we now call Iran, were about to invade **Attica** at a place near Athens called Marathon. The Persians had a huge army, and the Athenians decided to ask Sparta for help to fight them.

Pheidippides was chosen to take the message to Sparta, which was 125 km away. He was a trained runner, and he managed to reach Sparta in one day after leaving Athens.

Pheidippides claimed to have met Pan, the god of shepherds and herdsmen. Pan was usually pictured with a goat's horns, ears and legs. In this marble figure from the fifth century BC, he has lost one of his horns.

OTHER ATHLETES

Alcibiades (450–404 BC) – an Athenian statesman and general, who was also an excellent athlete.

24

The historian Herodotus reported that:

'The Spartans, though moved by the appeal, and willing to send help to Athens, were unable to send it promptly because they did not wish to break their law.'

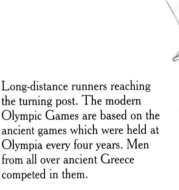

Long-distance runners reaching the turning post. The modern Olympic Games are based on the ancient games which were held at Olympia every four years. Men from all over ancient Greece competed in them.

Spartan law decreed that they were not allowed to march to battle until the moon was full. However, while returning home with this bad news, Pheidippides claimed that he met the god Pan on Mount Parthenion, who told him that he was on the Athenian side and would come and fight for them. Encouraged by this, the Athenians marched against the Persians and defeated them at the Battle of Marathon.

The place on Mount Parthenion where Pheidippides said he met Pan was made into a **shrine**, which attracted many visitors in ancient times. Pausanius, a travel writer, visiting nearly 650 years after the Battle of Marathon, wrote that:

'Parthenion has tortoises which are excellent for making lyres but the mountain people are always terrified to take them, nor do they let strangers catch them either; they believe the tortoises are sacred to Pan.'

Pheidippides ran 250 km in two days, and long-distance running races have been called marathons ever since.

DATE CHART

c.515 BC
Pheidippides is born.

500–499 BC
The Greek colonies in Ionia revolt against the Persians, but are defeated.

490 BC
Pheidippides runs to Sparta and back in two days.
Battle of Marathon.

480 BC
Second Persian invasion of Greece: Battle of Theropylae and the destruction of Athens.
***The Persians*, the first surviving play by Aeschylus, is performed.**

478 BC
Battle of Plataea: the Greeks defeat the Persian invasion.

465–330 BC
The Persian Empire declines and is eventually conquered by Alexander the Great.

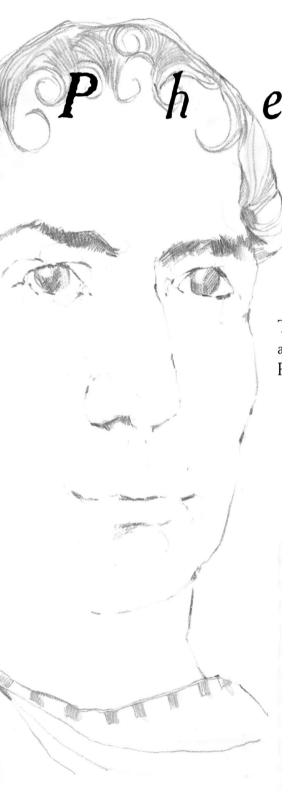

Pheidias

490-417 BC

'When the statue was completely finished, Pheidias prayed to the god to make a sign if the work pleased him, and immediately a flash of lightning struck the pavement...'

The statue was of the god Zeus. He was the father of the Greek gods, and was famous for throwing his thunderbolts around! So Pheidias (or Phidias) knew Zeus was pleased with his work.

This is a copy of Pheidias's statue of Zeus at Olympia. Pausanius wrote: 'Let a man sick and weary in his soul, who has passed through many distresses and sorrows, whose pillow is unvisited by kindly sleep, stand in front of this image; he will, I deem, forget all the troubles of human life.'

OTHER SCULPTORS

Praxiteles (fourth century BC) – his best-known statue is of the god Hermes carrying the infant god Dionysus.

Scopas (fourth century BC) – a sculptor and architect. He is famous for showing strong feelings in his sculptures.

Lysippus (fourth century BC) – Alexander the Great's court sculptor. None of his work has survived, but we know what it was like from Roman copies.

Part of the frieze on the Parthenon. It shows the great, four-yearly Panathenaic procession. This was when the Athenians went up to Athena's temple to present their goddess with a new robe.

This story was told by the travel writer Pausanius, when he visited Olympia. Here, where the original Olympic Games were held, was a shrine to Zeus, and inside his temple stood one of the wonders of the ancient world – Pheidias's huge statue of the god, covered in ivory and gold.

Pheidias came from Athens, and had a studio at Olympia. Athena was the special goddess of Athens. When Athena's temple was being rebuilt on the Acropolis after the Persian invasion, Pheidias was asked to decorate it and to make two statues of her. First he made a ten-metre bronze statue which stood at the huge marble gateway on the west side of the hill. The statue's helmet and lance flashing in the sun could be seen by boats far off at sea. Then Pheidias made another huge statue to go inside the temple. This one was made out of wood and covered with gold and ivory. He used gold for Athena's robes, and the ivory was used on her face, neck and arms to look like skin.

Pheidias's other great work was a marble **frieze**, the Elgin Marbles, that went all the way round the temple. It showed scenes from Greek myths of gods and goddesses, and a procession of the people of Athens.

Unfortunately, as Plutarch says:

'... the fame of Pheidias's works ... served to arouse jealousy against him ...'

Pheidias included pictures of himself and his friend Pericles, the leader of the Athenian government, amongst the figures in the scene on Athena's shield. Pericles' enemies were furious and accused Pheidias of stealing some of the gold that should have been used for the statue. Although he proved that the charges were false, Pheidias was thrown into prison, fell ill and died.

DATE CHART

c.490 BC
Pheidias is born.

480 BC
Athens is overcome by the Persians; the temples on the Acropolis are destroyed.

460–457 BC
The Long Walls are built around Athens. Pheidias is in charge of rebuilding the temples on the Acropolis.

449 BC
The Delian League makes peace with Persia.

443–429 BC
The Age of Pericles. He is elected Strategos every year.

431–404 BC
Peloponnesian War between Athens and Sparta.

430 BC
Athens is hit by a plague.

429 BC
Death of Pericles.

421 BC
Fifty years of peace between Athens and Sparta declared.

415 BC
Pheidias dies.

404 BC
Spartan victory over Athens. The Acropolis is destroyed and many of Pheidias's statues are taken as spoils of war.

Hippocrates

c. 470 – 400 BC

'With purity and with holiness I will pass my life and practise my Art.'

This is part of the Hippocratic Oath. It was a promise made by all students and followers of Hippocrates, the great **physician** of ancient Greece, and it is still made by some students of medicine to this day.

Hippocrates lived during the fifth century BC. At that time, if people fell ill they would go to the nearest *Asclepia*. This was a 'Temple of Health' where they would be tended by *Asclepiadae*, who were a cross between priests and doctors. At the entrance of the *Asclepia*, the patient would be cleaned, bathed using herbs in water, then put on a strict diet. He or she would then take part in religious ceremonies and do plenty of exercise, especially riding horses. Meanwhile the *Asclepiadae* would take careful notes about the progress of the disease.

Hippocrates was one of the *Asclepiadae* at the famous *Asclepia* on the island of Cos. He probably inherited the position from his father, and learnt about medicine from him and from the large collection of notes at the temple. However, Hippocrates did not believe that illnesses were inflicted by the gods; he knew that they could all be traced to natural causes. For example, **epilepsy** was called the 'Sacred Disease' at that time, because it was thought to be a punishment from the gods. But Hippocrates wrote:

'Men regard its nature and cause as divine from ignorance and wonder...'

The baths at the *Asclepia* at Cos. Bathing was believed to be an important part of the healing process.

He did not believe the 'cures' that some physicians recommended to their patients with epilepsy. For example, they would tell them not to bathe, nor to eat certain foods such as goat, eel, dog, mint or garlic, nor to wear a black robe. And certainly not to:

'...sleep on a goat's skin, or to wear it, or to put one foot on another, or one hand on another...'

People who were cured often left a model of their affected body part, such as this wooden leg, as an offering of thanks to Asclepius, the god of medicine.

Hippocrates studied his patients and their diseases very carefully, and wrote several books which laid the foundations of modern medicine. Athletes would often injure themselves at the games, and Hippocrates became expert at healing broken limbs and bones which had come out of place. He was also a fearless surgeon, and would operate boldly on the skull if someone had a head injury. His fame spread quickly and he travelled all over Greece to heal people. It is said that he cured King Perdiccas of Macedonia of love-sickness.

30

There were no anaesthetics, so operations were dangerous and very painful. This carving shows a case of surgical instruments. On either side are cups which were used for collecting blood from the patients.

Athens during this period had been struck by the plague, and it is said that Hippocrates cured the city of the disease by lighting fires around it. By separating medicine from superstition and treating it as a science, Hippocrates earned his reputation throughout the ages as 'The Father of Medicine'. For example, his theory of bodily 'humours', or fluids in the body which caused different moods, was seen as an important medical fact for many years, almost until the twentieth century.

Socrates

469 - 399 BC

'... the best and wisest and most righteous man.'

Socrates' pupil, Plato, wrote this about him after his death.

Socrates was one of the famous philosophers of Athens. He led a simple life, scorning wealth and accepting no payment for his teaching. He taught **philosophy** and the art of speaking in public, and believed that knowledge made people good and ignorance made them bad.

A statue of Socrates. The historian Xenophon said of him: 'He seemed to me to be the perfect example of goodness and happiness.'

Unfortunately, Socrates often made people angry. For example, he believed strongly in democracy and found himself in trouble when he defied the orders of the ruling **Thirty Tyrants**. But his main problem was that the people of Athens did not like him thinking he was better than they were. A character in a comedy by Aristophanes says of him:

'You strut along the streets, and look around you proudly,
And barefoot many ills endure, and hold your head above us.'

33

This carving shows Socrates' death scene. The woman on the left may be his wife Xanthippe, although we know from Plato's account that Socrates sent her away from his death-bed because he could not bear her crying.

However, an oracle, or a message from the gods, was believed to have said:

'Socrates of all mortals is the wisest.'

This was more than his enemies could bear, and Socrates was charged with 'introducing strange gods' and corrupting young people. He was found guilty. While the court was discussing how much to fine him, he said:

'My real opinion is that, as a return for what has been done by me, I deserve to be paid by the state for the rest of my life.'

The court did not find this very funny, and he was sentenced to death. Some days later he was made to drink hemlock, a type of poison, and died.

Socrates never wrote down his ideas. They were reported by Plato, who founded a school of philosophy outside Athens. The school lasted for 800 years. Socrates' ideas have had a great influence on the Western world, right up until the present century.

Socrates' pupil and friend, Plato. He wrote the *Apology* defending Socrates and many *Dialogues* which set out Socrates' teaching.

DATE CHART

469 BC
Socrates is born.

443–429 BC
The Age of Pericles.

431–404 BC
The Peloponnesian War, fought between Athens and Sparta.

404 BC
Spartan victory over Athens in the Peloponnesian War. Athens is forced to accept the government of the Thirty Tyrants.

403 BC
Democracy is brought back to Athens.

399 BC
Wars between Sparta and Persia begin. Socrates is condemned to death by drinking hemlock.

35

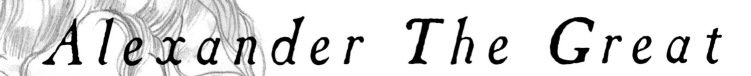

Alexander The Great

356 - 323 BC

'Alexander did not want to inherit a kingdom that would bring him wealth, luxury and pleasure; but one that would afford him wars, conflicts and all the exercise of great ambition.'

There are so many stories about Alexander the Great, who is described above by Plutarch, that it is difficult to know what is true and what is legend. Alexander was the son of King Philip of Macedon. He was very striking to look at, with a mane of hair like a lion and different-coloured eyes – some accounts say one was black and one white. Also, it was said that:

This coin, from about 3 BC, shows Alexander's head.

36

'... a most agreeable scent proceeded from his skin, and his breath and whole body were so fragrant that they perfumed his underwear.'

As a boy he was believed to have amazed everyone by taming a man-eating horse and riding it around the town, although this is probably a myth.

Alexander became king at the age of twenty, after his father was murdered. He had already found fame as a fearless and clever soldier, and almost immediately after his father's death he began a campaign to enlarge his kingdom. Philip had conquered a large area of Europe and some of these states hoped, at his death, to become independent again. But Alexander soon crushed that hope and dealt ruthlessly with the rebel states. When he overcame the town of Thebes, 6,000 people were killed and the rest were sold into slavery. He then burned the city down.

Alexander leading his troops on his horse. As a young man he worried that his father would 'go on conquering until there is nothing extraordinary left for me to do'.

Most of Alexander's troops were heavily armoured foot soldiers like this, known as *hoplites*.

DATE CHART

356 BC
Alexander is born.

359 BC
Philip II becomes King of Macedonia.

340 BC
Greek states form the Hellenic League against Philip.

338 BC
Philip defeats the Hellenic League and becomes ruler of Greece.

337 BC
Philip, with all the Greek states, declares war on Persia.

336 BC
Death of Philip. Alexander becomes king.

335 BC
Alexander crushes Thebes.

334 BC
Alexander attacks the Persians.

333 BC
Alexander defeats the Persians at the Battle of Issus.

332 BC
Alexander conquers Phoenicia, Samaria, Judaea, Gaza and Egypt. He founds the city of Alexandria.

331 BC
Alexander defeats the Persians and becomes King of Persia.

327 BC
Alexander advances into India.

326 BC
Alexander defeats the Indian King Porus at the battle of the River Hydaspes.

323 BC
Alexander dies.

Once he had Europe under control, Alexander started a war against Persia. For eleven years he advanced across Asia, finally taking the Persian capital, Persepolis, and proclaiming himself King of Persia.

One of the towns Alexander marched through was Gordius, the capital of the ancient kingdom of Phrygia. In the ruins of the palace there was a chariot tied to a pole with a very complicated knot. There was a **prophecy** which said that whoever untied the knot would become king of all Asia. Alexander tried to undo the knot, but failed. He then took out his sword and cut through the knot, so fulfilling the prophecy. 'To cut the Gordian knot' is still a well-known saying, meaning to find a way out of a difficulty.

Through his brilliance as a general, Alexander went on to conquer Egypt and advanced through India. But his troops would go no further and he had to return. Everywhere he went he founded new cities. The most famous of these is Alexandria in Egypt, which has continued to be an important port for the last 2,000 years.

When Alexander set out, he had seen himself as a champion of the Greeks against the **barbarians,** or uncivilized peoples. The Greeks regarded the Asians as barbarians, but on his travels Alexander seems to have changed his mind. He formed the idea of an **empire**, where he would rule over Europeans and Asians as equals. He founded cities peopled by a mixture of Greeks, Macedonians and Persians, and encouraged mixed marriages. Alexander himself followed the Persian custom of having more than one wife, and married three times. He even began to wear the robes of a Persian king for court ceremonies.

Alexander the Great's Asian empire did not last long, however. He was preparing to invade Arabia when he caught a fever. He was only thirty-two years old when he died, but in his short life he had conquered the largest empire in the ancient world and had spread Greek culture across many lands.

Alexander's fame spread throughout Asia, and stories were still told about him thousands of years after his death. This picture of him illustrates a book from 1531 and shows him in his Persian robes.

OTHER MILITARY LEADERS

Philip of Macedon (382–336 BC) – the father of Alexander. He made Macedonia a major power and became leader of all the Greeks.

Ptolemy I (c.370–283 BC) – a Macedonian general who later became King of Egypt.

Seleucus I (c.360–280 BC) – a Macedonian general who seized a large part of Alexander's empire and became one of the three main rulers of the ancient Greek lands.

Archimedes

c. 287 – 212 BC

'Give me a place to stand and I will move the Earth.'

Archimedes made this boast because he had realized the power of machines, especially **levers**, to lift heavy objects.

Archimedes lived in Syracuse, in Sicily. Hiero, the King of Syracuse, often asked for his help to get out of difficulties. For example, one of King Hiero's ships kept filling up with water and sinking, so he asked Archimedes to find a way of getting the water out. Archimedes invented a machine for doing this which was called an 'Archimedes' screw'. Machines based on this are still used today for lifting water.

An Archimedes' screw being used in present-day Egypt to lift water past a dam.

One day, King Hiero asked Archimedes to solve a difficult problem. A jeweller had made him a crown which he said was made of pure gold. Hiero suspected that he had been cheated and that there was silver underneath the gold. He asked Archimedes to find a way to tell if this was true. Archimedes thought about it for a long time, then one day he got into his bath. This was an unusual event – he used to think so hard about his mathematical investigations that he would forget to eat or wash and often had to be forced to have a bath. Even then he would write sums in the ashes of the fire next to his bath and draw diagrams on his wet skin. But when he got into the bath on this particular day, he noticed that the water level rose. Suddenly he found the answer to the problem. He realized that the amount of water that an object **displaces** is the same as the **volume** of the object, so he could measure the volume of King Hiero's crown by putting it in water. He was so excited that he leapt out of the bath and ran through the streets naked, shouting 'heureka!', which means 'I have found it!'.

The goldsmith had been given a lump of gold with which to make the crown. Archimedes found that an identical lump of gold weighed the same as the crown. But when he put them both in water, the crown displaced more water than the gold. The crown, therefore, had a larger volume than the lump of gold. The goldsmith had kept some of this gold for himself. Because gold is denser than silver, he had added extra silver under a thin layer of gold to make up the weight of the crown.

DATE CHART

c.300 BC
Euclid writes his book on geometry, *The Elements*.

c.287 BC
Archimedes is born.

273–192 BC
Eratosthenes measures the Earth's size and maps the known world.

212 BC
The Romans capture Syracuse. Archimedes dies.

c.200 BC
Hipparchus studies the planets, makes an accurate star map and estimates the distance between the Earth and the Sun.

41

The Romans learned a great deal about mechanics from Archimedes. This Roman monument from about 1 BC shows people using a hoist and treadmill.

OTHER SCIENTISTS

Pythagoras (c.580–500 BC) – a mathematician who discovered rules that are still used in maths today, such as Pythagoras' Theorem.

Thales of Miletus (c.625–545 BC) – a mathematician who calculated the height of a pyramid by measuring its shadow.

Euclid (third century BC) – a mathematician who worked out and wrote down many rules of geometry and maths.

Archimedes' inventions were very useful when the Romans tried to capture Syracuse. By using levers and pulleys, he invented huge catapults and machines that could lift the enemy ships up out of the water and drop them again, smashing them to bits. Plutarch said that:

'At last the Romans were so terrified, that if they saw but a rope or a stick put over the walls, they cried out that Archimedes was levelling some machine at them, and turned their backs and fled.'

But finally, after besieging the town for three years, the Romans captured it. A Roman soldier, finding Archimedes working on a maths problem, tried to take him to the victorious general. Archimedes refused to go, saying that he had to solve his problem first. The soldier was so angry that he killed him.

Archimedes was the greatest mathematician of the Western world, and he is known as the 'Father of Mechanics' (the science of machines).

Discover the Power of Levers for Yourself

– use one coin to lift two.

You will need a pencil, a ruler and a few coins of the same kind.

1. Put the pencil on a table and balance the ruler on it to make a see-saw.

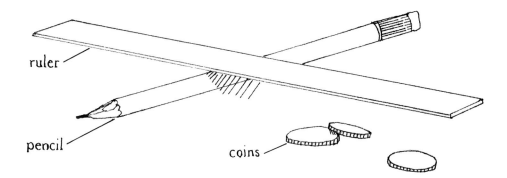

2. Put two coins together on the ruler, 2 cm away from the pencil. Put one coin exactly the same distance from the pencil on the other side.

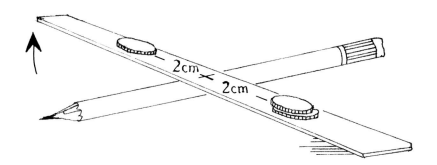

3. Now move the single coin slowly away from the pencil. At what point does the ruler balance? Can you see how you have used just one coin to lift two?

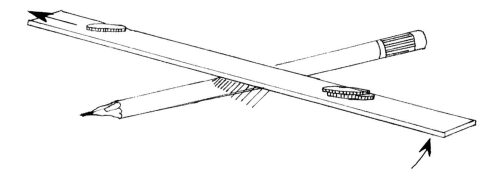

Glossary

Acropolis The word means 'high city' in Greek. It is the part of Athens on which the Parthenon stands, above the rest of the city.

Archon One of the chief officials of Athens.

Attica The state made up of Athens and the surrounding countryside.

Barbarians The name given by the Greeks to anyone who was foreign to them.

Besiege To surround a city with military forces to try to make the people inside surrender.

Delian League The league of Greek states, led by Athens, which was formed between 478 and 449 BC to protect its members from the Persians.

Delphi The site of the Temple of Apollo, the most famous oracle in Greece.

Democracy A system in which all citizens have a say in the government of their state or country.

Deserter Someone who runs away from the army.

Displace To cause a quantity of liquid to move.

Empire A group of countries under one ruler.

Epilepsy An illness in which the patient can have fits or can fall to the ground unconscious.

Exile When a person is banished from a country.

Fertile Able to produce a good crop.

Frieze A band of decoration, painting or sculpture.

Geometry A type of maths involving the study of lines, angles, surfaces and solid shapes.

Hellenic League A group of Greek states formed in 342 BC to oppose Philip of Macedon.

Lawgiver Someone who makes laws.

Lever A simple machine used for lifting weights.

Long Walls The great walls that linked Athens to its port at Piraeus from 460 to 404 BC.

Lyre A stringed instrument, made from a tortoise shell and the horns of an ox.

Mummified When a body is dried and made to last a long time by covering it with oils.

Oracle A sacred place, usually a temple, where people went to ask the advice of a god or goddess.

Peloponnesian War The war between Sparta and Athens that lasted for twenty-seven years, between 431 and 404 BC.

Philosopher A scholar who studies and tries to understand the world around him or her.

Philosophy The search for the truth about life.

Physician A healer, either a doctor or a surgeon.

Plague A serious infectious disease.

Prophecy A prediction of something that will happen in the future.

Seven Wise Men These are believed to have been Bias, Chilon of Sparta, Cleobulus, Periander, Pittacus, Solon and Thales of Miletus.

Shrine A place which is sacred to the memory of someone, usually a god or goddess.

Strategos One of ten powerful army commanders who were elected each year in Athens.

Thirty Tyrants After Sparta had defeated Athens at the end of the Peloponnesian War, the Spartans installed a government at Athens called the Thirty Tyrants. 'Tyrant' meant 'ruler' in ancient Greek, but it has since come to mean a cruel ruler.

Trilogy Three plays which are performed one after the other.

Volume The amount of space that is taken up by an object.

Books to read

John Ellis Jones, *Ancient Greece* (Kingfisher, 1992)
Anne Pearson, *Ancient Greece* (Dorling Kindersley
  Eyewitness Guide, 1992)

Susan Peach & Anne Millard, *The Greeks*
  (Usborne, 1990)
Peter Lafferty, *Archimedes* (Wayland, 1991)

Places to visit

You can see ancient Greek art and artefacts at the following places:

Birmingham City Museum, Birmingham.
Tel: (021) 235 3890
Fitzwilliam Museum, Cambridge.
Tel: (0223) 337733/332900
Museum of Classical Archaeology, Cambridge.
Tel: (0223) 62253 ext. 29
Cheltenham Borough Council Art Gallery and
Museum Service, Cheltenham. Tel: (0242) 237431
Royal Museum of Scotland, Edinburgh.
Tel: (031) 225 7534
City Art Gallery, Leeds. Tel: (0532) 462495
Liverpool Museum, Liverpool.
Tel: (051) 207 0001
British Museum, London. Tel: 071 636 1555
Greek Museum, University of Newcastle, Newcastle
Upon Tyne. Tel: (0632) 328511 ext. 3966

Ashmolean Museum, Oxford. Tel: (0865) 512651
The Ure Museum of Greek Archaeology, University
of Reading, Whiteknights, Reading.
Tel: (0734) 875123 ext. 269/358

Many local museums or art galleries may also have
ancient Greek exhibits.

I n d e x